The Art of Living

The Classical Manual on Virtue Happiness, and Effectiveness

A New Interpretation by Sharon Lebell

HarperOne
An Imprint of HarperCollins*Publishers*

For John, Keilah, Misha, and Danya,
and thanks to Bernard and Lyla Grossman.

HarperOne

The section of this book entitled "A Manual for Living" sub-
stantially reproduces the main text of the book Epictetus,
A *Manual for Living*, A New Interpretation by Sharon Lebell,
copyright © 1994 by HarperCollins Publishers and is used
here by permission.
Epigraph from Epictetus *Discourses*, 3.23, tr. Thomas W.
Higginson (Roslyn, New York: Walter J. Black, 1944), 233.

Library of Congress Cataloging-in-Publication Data
is available.
ISBN 978–0–06–128605–6
ISBN-10: 0–06–128605–2

17 18 19 20   LSCC   30 29 28 27

Contents

Essential Teachings on
Virtue, Happiness, and Tranquility   81

Part of Epictetus's enduring appeal and widespread influence is that he wasn't fussy about distinguishing between professional philosophers and ordinary people. He expressed his message clearly and zealously to all people interested in living a morally awake life.

Epictetus nevertheless staunchly believed in the necessity of training for the gradual refinement of personal character and behavior. Moral progress is not the natural province of the highborn, nor is it achieved by accident or luck, but by working on yourself—daily.

Epictetus would have had little patience for the aggressive position-taking and -defending and verbal pirouettes that unfortunately sometimes pass for "doing" philosophy in today's universities. As a master of succinct explanation, he would have been similarly suspicious of the murky verbiage found in academic, philosophical, and other dry texts. Inasmuch as he passionately denounced displays of cleverness for its own sake, he was committed to non-patronizing explanations of helpful ideas for living well. He considered himself successful when his ideas were easily grasped and *put to use* in someone's real life, where they could actually do some good elevating that person's character.

In keeping with the democratic and unstuffy spirit of Epictetus's doctrine, this volume encapsulates the great Stoic's key ideas and uses down-to-earth language and imagery suited to our ears today. To present Epictetus's teachings in as straightforward and useful a manner as possible, I have done my share of selection, interpretation, and improvisation with the ideas contained in the *Enchiridion* and the *Discourses*, the only surviving documents that summarize Epictetus's philosophy. My aim has been to communicate the authentic spirit, but not necessarily the letter, of Epictetus. I have thus consulted the various translations of his teachings and then given fresh expression to what I think he would have said today.

Epictetus well understood the eloquence of action. He exhorted his students to shun mere clever theorizing in favor of actively applying his teachings to the concrete circumstances of daily life. Accordingly, I have tried to express the kernels of Epictetus's thought in an up-to-date, provocative way, one that will inspire readers not only to contemplate, but to make the small, successive changes that culminate in personal dignity and a meaningful, noble life.

How do I live a happy, fulfilling life?

How can I be a good person?

Answering these two questions was the single-minded passion of Epictetus, the great Stoic philosopher. Although his works are less well-known today, due to the decline of classical education, they have had enormous influence on leading thinkers on the art of living for almost two millennia.

Epictetus was born a slave about A.D. 55 in Hierapolis, Phrygia, in the eastern outreaches of the Roman Empire. His master was Epaphroditus, Nero's administrative secretary. From an early age, Epictetus exhibited superior intellectual talent, and Epaphroditus was so impressed that he sent the young man to Rome to study with the famous Stoic teacher, Gaius Musonius Rufus. Musonius Rufus's works, which survive in Greek, include arguments in favor of equal education for women and against the sexual double standard in marriage, and Epictetus's famous egalitarian spirit may have been nurtured under his tutelage. Epictetus became Musonius Rufus's most acclaimed student and was eventually freed from slavery.

Epictetus taught in Rome until A.D. 94, when the emperor Domitian, threatened by the growing influence of philosophers, banished him from Rome. He spent the rest of his life in exile in Nicopolis, on the northwest coast of Greece. There he established a philosophical school, and spent his days delivering lectures on how to live with greater dignity and tranquility. Among his most distinguished students was the young Marcus Aurelius Antoninus, who eventually became ruler of the Roman Empire. He was also the author of the famous *Meditations*, whose Stoic roots were in Epictetus's moral doctrines.

Even though Epictetus was a brilliant master of logic and disputation, he didn't flaunt his exceptional rhetorical skill. His demeanor was that of a lighthearted, humble teacher urging his students to take the business of living wisely very seriously. Epictetus walked his talk: He lived modestly in a small hut and eschewed any interest in fame, fortune, and power. He died about A.D. 135, in Nicopolis.

Epictetus believed that the primary job of philosophy is to help ordinary people effectively meet the everyday challenges of daily life, and to deal with life's inevitable major losses, disappointments, and griefs. His was a moral teaching stripped of sentimentality, piousness, and metaphysical mumbo-jumbo. What remains is the West's first and best primer for living the best possible life.

While many readers have turned to Eastern sources for nonsectarian spiritual guidance, the West has had a vital, if overlooked, classic treasury of such helpful action-wisdom all along. One of the wittiest teachers who ever lived, Epictetus's teachings rank with those contained in the greatest wisdom literature of human civilization. The *Discourses* could be thought of as the West's answer to Buddhism's *Dhammapada* or Lao Tzu's *Tao Te Ching*. Those who fault Western philosophy with being overly cerebral and inadequately addressing the nonrational dimensions of life may be surprised to learn that *The Art of Living* is actually a philosophy of inner freedom and tranquility, a way of life whose purpose is to lighten our hearts.

An unexpectedly East-West flavor enlivens *The Art of Living*. On the one hand, its style is irrefutably Western: It exalts reason and is full of stern, no-nonsense moral directives. On the other hand, a soft Easterly wind seems to blow when Epictetus discusses the nature of the universe. His depiction of Ultimate Reality, for instance, which he equates with Nature itself, is remarkably fluid and elusive: startlingly reminiscent of the Tao.

For Epictetus, a happy life and a virtuous life are synonymous. Happiness and personal fulfillment are the natural consequences of doing the right thing. Unlike many philosophers of his day, Epictetus was less concerned with seeking to understand the world than with identifying the specific steps to take in the pursuit of moral excellence. Part of his genius is his emphasis on moral *progress* over the seeking of moral *perfection*. With a keen understanding of how easily we human beings are diverted from living by our highest principles, he exhorts us to view the philosophical life as a progression of steps that gradually approximates our cherished personal ideals.

Epictetus's notion of the good life is not a matter of following a laundry list of precepts, but of bringing our actions and desires into harmony with nature. The point is not to perform good deeds to win favor with the gods or the admiration of others, but to achieve inner serenity and thus enduring personal freedom. Goodness is an equal opportunity enterprise, available to *anyone* at any time: rich or poor, educated or simple. It is not the exclusive province of "spiritual professionals," such as monks, saints, or ascetics.

Epictetus advanced a conception of virtue that was simple, ordinary, and day-to-day in its expression. He favored a life lived steadily in accordance with the divine will over extraordinary, conspicuous, heroic displays of goodness. His prescription for the good life centered on three main themes: mastering your desires, performing your duties, and learning to think clearly about yourself and your relations within the larger community of humanity.

Epictetus recognized that everyday life is fraught with difficulties of varying degree. He spent his life outlining the path to happiness, fulfillment, and tranquility, no matter what one's circumstances happen to be. His teachings, when freed of their ancient cultural trappings, have an uncanny contemporary relevance. At times, his philosophy sounds like the best of contemporary psychology. The Serenity Prayer, which epitomizes the recovery movement—"Grant me the serenity to accept the things I cannot change, the courage to change the things I can, and the wisdom to know the difference"—could easily be a sentence in this book. In fact, Epictetus's thought is one of the taproots of the modern psychology of self-management.

In other important ways, however, Epictetus is very traditional and uncontemporary. Whereas our society (practically, if not always explicitly) regards professional achievement, wealth, power, and fame as desirable and admirable, Epictetus views these as incidental and irrelevant to true happiness. What matters most is what sort of person you are becoming, what sort of life you are living.

First, say to yourself what you would be;
then do what you have to do.

The *Manual*

Epictetus was a lecturer who left no philosophical writings. Fortunately, the main points of his philosophy were preserved for future generations by his devoted pupil, the historian Flavius Arrian. Arrian painstakingly transcribed a large number of his teacher's lectures in Greek for a friend. These lectures, known as the *Discourses* (or *Diatribes*), were originally collected in eight books, but only four survive. Epictetus's lectures are among the major sources for our present-day understanding of Roman Stoic philosophy.

Epictetus's *Manual* (or *Enchiridion*) is a pithy set of excerpts selected from the *Discourses* that forms a concise summary of Epictetus's essential teachings. It was roughly modeled on military manuals of the day and thus shares some of the bold simplicity of such classics as *The Art of War*. (Soldiers even carried the *Manual* into battle.) Across centuries and cultures, world leaders, generals, and ordinary folk alike have relied on the *Manual* as their main guide to personal serenity and moral direction amid the trials of life.

Know What You Can
Control and What You Can't

Happiness and freedom begin with a clear understanding of one principle: Some things are within our control, and some things are not. It is only after you have faced up to this fundamental rule and learned to distinguish between what you can and can't control that inner tranquility and outer effectiveness become possible.

Within our control are our own opinions, aspirations, desires, and the things that repel us. These areas are quite rightly our concern, because they are directly subject to our influence. We always have a choice about the contents and character of our inner lives.

Outside our control, however, are such things as what kind of body we have, whether we're born into wealth or strike it rich, how we are regarded by others, and our status in society. We must remember that those things are externals and are therefore not our concern. Trying to control or to change what we can't only results in torment.

Remember: The things within our power are naturally at our disposal, free from any restraint or hindrance; but those things outside our power are weak, dependent, or determined by the whims and actions of others. Remember, too, that if you think that you have free rein over things that are naturally beyond your control, or if you attempt to adopt the affairs of others as your own, your pursuits will be thwarted and you will become a frustrated, anxious, and fault-finding person.

Keep your attention focused entirely on what is truly your own concern, and be clear that what belongs to others is their business and none of yours. If you do this, you will be impervious to coercion and no one can ever hold you back. You will be truly free and effective, for your efforts will be put to good use and won't be foolishly squandered finding fault with or opposing others.

In knowing and attending to what actually concerns you, you cannot be made to do anything against your will; others can't hurt you, you don't incur enemies or suffer harm.

If you aim to live by such principles, remember that it won't be easy: you must give up some things entirely, and postpone others for now. You may well have to forego wealth and power if you want to assure the attainment of happiness and freedom.

Recognize Appearances for What They Really Are

From now on, practice saying to everything that appears unpleasant: "You are just an appearance and by no means what you appear to be." And then thoroughly consider the matter according to the principles just discussed, primarily: Does this appearance concern the things that are within my own control or those that are not? If it concerns anything outside your control, train yourself not to worry about it.

Our desires and aversions are mercurial rulers. They demand to be pleased. Desire commands us to run off and get what we want. Aversion insists that we must avoid the things that repel us.

Typically, when we don't get what we want, we are disappointed, and when we get what we don't want, we are distressed.

If, then, you avoid only those undesirable things that are contrary to your natural well-being and are within your control, you won't ever incur anything you truly don't want. However, if you try to avoid inevitabilities such as sickness, death, or misfortune, over which you have no real control, you will make yourself and others around you suffer.

Desire and aversion, though powerful, are but habits. And we can train ourselves to have better habits. Restrain the habit of being repelled by all those things that aren't within your control, and focus instead on combating things within your power that are not good for you.

Do your best to rein in your desire. For if you desire something that isn't within your own control, disappointment will surely follow; meanwhile, you will be neglecting the very things that are within your control that are worthy of desire.

Of course, there are times when for practical reasons you must go after one thing or shun another, but do so with grace, finesse, and flexibility.

See Things for What They Are

Circumstances do not rise to meet our expectations. Events happen as they do. People behave as they are. Embrace what you actually get.

Open your eyes: See things for what they really are, thereby sparing yourself the pain of false attachments and avoidable devastation.

Think about what delights you—the tools on which you depend, the people whom you cherish. But remember that they have their own distinct character, which is quite a separate matter from how we happen to regard them.

As an exercise, consider the smallest things to which you are attached. For instance, suppose you have a favorite cup. It is, after all, merely a cup; so if it should break, you could cope. Next build up to things—or people—toward which your clinging feelings and thoughts intensify.

Remember, for example, when you embrace your child, your husband, your wife, you are embracing a mortal. Thus, if one of them should die, you could bear it with tranquility.

When something happens, the only thing in your power is your attitude toward it; you can either accept it or resent it.

What really frightens and dismays us is not external events themselves, but the way in which we think about them. It is not things that disturb us, but our interpretation of their significance.

Stop scaring yourself with impetuous notions, with your reactive impressions of the way things are!

Things and people are not what we wish them to be nor what they seem to be. They are what they are.

Don't try to make your own rules.

Conduct yourself in all matters, grand and public or small and domestic, in accordance with the laws of nature. Harmonizing your will with nature should be your utmost ideal.

Where do you practice this ideal? In the particulars of your own daily life with its uniquely personal tasks and duties. When you carry out your tasks, such as taking a bath, do so—to the best of your ability—in harmony with nature. When you eat, do so—to the best of your ability— in harmony with nature, and so on.

It is not so much what you are doing as how you are doing it. When we properly understand and live by this principle, while difficulties will arise— for they are part of the divine order too—inner peace will still be possible.

Things themselves don't hurt or hinder us. Nor do other people. How we view these things is another matter. It is our attitudes and reactions that give us trouble.

Therefore even death is no big deal in and of itself. It is our notion of death, our idea that it is terrible, that terrifies us. There are so many different ways to think about death. Scrutinize your notions about death—and everything else. Are they really true? Are they doing you any good? Don't dread death or pain; dread the fear of death or pain.

We cannot choose our external circumstances, but we can always choose how we respond to them.

If it is our feelings about things that torment us rather than the things themselves, it follows that blaming others is silly. Therefore, when we suffer setbacks, disturbances, or grief, let us never place the blame on others, but on our own attitudes.

Small-minded people habitually reproach others for their own misfortunes. Average people reproach themselves. Those who are dedicated to a life of wisdom understand that the impulse to blame something or someone is foolishness, that there is nothing to be gained in blaming, whether it be others or oneself.

One of the signs of the dawning of moral progress is the gradual extinguishing of blame. We see the futility of finger-pointing. The more we examine our attitudes and work on ourselves, the less we are apt to be swept away by stormy emotional reactions in which we seek easy explanations for unbidden events.

Things simply are what they are. Other people think what they will think; it is of no concern to us. No Shame. No Blame.

Never depend on the admiration of others. There is no strength in it. Personal merit cannot be derived from an external source. It is not to be found in your personal associations, nor can it be found in the regard of other people. It is a fact of life that other people, even people who love you, will not necessarily agree with your ideas, understand you, or share your enthusiasms. Grow up! Who cares what other people think about you!

Create your *own* merit.

Personal merit cannot be achieved through our associations with people of excellence. You have been given your own work to do. Get to it right now, do your best at it, and don't be concerned with who is watching you.

Do your own useful work without regard to the honor or admiration your efforts might win from others. There is no such thing as vicarious merit.

Other people's triumphs and excellences belong to them. Likewise, your possessions may have excellence, but you yourself don't derive excellence from them.

Think about it: What is really your own? The use you make of the ideas, resources, and opportunities that come your way. Do you have books? Read them. Learn from them. Apply their wisdom. Do you have specialized knowledge? Put it to its full and good use. Do you have tools? Get them out and build or repair things with them. Do you have a good idea? Follow up and follow through on it. Make the most of what you've got, what is actually yours.

You can be justifiably happy with yourself and at ease when you've harmonized your actions with nature by recognizing what truly is your own.

There is a time and place for diversion and amusements, but you should never allow them to override your true purposes. If you were on a voyage and the ship anchored in a harbor, you might go ashore for water and happen to pick up a shellfish or a plant. But be careful; listen for the call of the captain. Keep your attention directed at the ship. Getting distracted by trifles is the easiest thing in the world. Should the captain call, you must be ready to leave those distractions and come running, without even looking back.

If you are old, do not go far from the ship, or you might fail to appear when you are called for.

Accept Events As They Occur

Don't demand or expect that events happen as you would wish them to. Accept events as they actually happen. That way peace is possible.

Nothing truly stops you. Nothing truly holds you back. For your own will is always within your control.

Sickness may challenge your body. But are you merely your body? Lameness may impede your legs. But you are not merely your legs. Your will is bigger than your legs.

Your will needn't be affected by an incident unless you let it. Remember this with everything that happens to you.

Every difficulty in life presents us with an opportunity to turn inward and to invoke our own submerged inner resources. The trials we endure can and should introduce us to our strengths.

Prudent people look beyond the incident itself and seek to form the habit of putting it to good use.

On the occasion of an accidental event, don't just react in a haphazard fashion: Remember to turn inward and ask what resources you have for dealing with it. Dig deeply. You possess strengths you might not realize you have. Find the right one. Use it.

If you encounter an attractive person, then self-restraint is the resource needed; if pain or weakness, then stamina; if verbal abuse, then patience.

As time goes by and you build on the habit of matching the appropriate inner resource to each incident, you will not tend to get carried away by life's appearances. You will stop feeling overwhelmed so much of the time.

Nothing can truly be taken from us. There is nothing to lose. Inner peace begins when we stop saying of things, "I have lost it" and instead say, "It has been returned to where it came from." Have your children died? They are returned to where they came from. Has your mate died? Your mate is returned to where he or she came from. Have your possessions and property been taken from you? They too have been returned to where they came from.

Perhaps you are vexed because a bad person took your belongings. But why should it be any concern of yours who gives your things back to the world that gave them to you?

The important thing is to take great care with what you have while the world lets you have it, just as a traveler takes care of a room at an inn.

The surest sign of the higher life is serenity. Moral progress results in freedom from inner turmoil. You can stop fretting about this and that.

If you seek the higher life, refrain from such common patterns of thinking as these: "If I don't work harder, I'll never earn a decent living, no one will recognize me, I'll be a nobody," or "If I don't criticize my employee, he'll take advantage of my good will."

It's much better to die of hunger unhindered by grief and fear than to live affluently beset with worry, dread, suspicion, and unchecked desire.

Begin at once a program of self-mastery. But start modestly, with the little things that bother you. Has your child spilled something? Have you misplaced your wallet? Say to yourself, "Coping calmly with this inconvenience is the price I pay for my inner serenity, for freedom from perturbation; you don't get something for nothing."

When you call your child, be prepared that she may not respond to you, or if she does, she might not do what you want her to do. Under these circumstances, it doesn't help your child for you to become agitated. It should not be in her power to cause you any disturbance.

Disregard What Doesn't Concern You

Spiritual progress requires us to highlight what is essential and to disregard everything else as trivial pursuits unworthy of our attention. Moreover, it is actually a good thing to be thought foolish and simple with regard to matters that don't concern us. Don't be concerned with other people's impressions of you. They are dazzled and deluded by appearances. Stick with your purpose. This alone will strengthen your will and give your life coherence.

Refrain from trying to win other people's approval and admiration. You are taking a higher road. Don't long for others to see you as sophisticated, unique, or wise. In fact, be suspicious if you appear to others as someone special. Be on your guard against a false sense of self-importance.

Keeping your will in harmony with truth and concerning yourself with what is beyond your control are mutually exclusive. While you are absorbed in one, you will neglect the other.

For good or for ill, life and nature are governed by laws that we can't change. The quicker we accept this, the more tranquil we can be. You would be foolish to wish that your children or your spouse would live forever. They are mortal, just as you are, and the law of mortality is completely out of your hands.

Similarly, it is foolish to wish that an employee, relative, or friend be without fault. This is wishing to control things that you can't truly control.

It is within our control not to be disappointed by our desires if we deal with them according to facts rather than by being swept away by them.

We are ultimately controlled by that which bestows what we seek or removes what we don't want. If it's freedom you seek, then wish nothing and shun nothing that depends on others, or you will always be a helpless slave.

Understand what freedom really is and how it is achieved. Freedom isn't the right or ability to do whatever you please. Freedom comes from understanding the limits of our own power and the natural limits set in place by divine providence. By accepting life's limits and inevitabilities and working with them rather than fighting them, we become free. If, on the other hand, we succumb to our passing desires for things that aren't in our control, freedom is lost.

Think of your life as if it were a banquet where you would behave graciously. When dishes are passed to you, extend your hand and help yourself to a moderate portion. If a dish should pass you by, enjoy what is already on your plate. Or if the dish hasn't been passed to you yet, patiently wait your turn.

Carry over this same attitude of polite restraint and gratitude to your children, spouse, career, and finances. There is no need to yearn, envy, and grab. You will get your rightful portion when it is your time.

Diogenes and Heraclitus were impeccable models of living by such principles rather than by raw impulses. Make it your quest to imitate their worthy example.

Other people's views and troubles can be contagious. Don't sabotage yourself by unwittingly adopting negative, unproductive attitudes through your associations with others.

If you encounter a downhearted friend, a grieving parent, or a colleague who has suffered a sudden reversal of fortune, be careful not to be overcome yourself by the apparent misfortune. Remember to discriminate between events themselves and your interpretations of them. Remind yourself: "What hurts this person is not the occurrence itself, for another person might not feel oppressed by this situation at all. What is hurting this person is the response he or she has uncritically adopted."

It is not a demonstration of kindness or friendship to the people we care about to join them in indulging in wrongheaded, negative feelings. We do a better service to ourselves and others by remaining detached and avoiding melodramatic reactions.

Still, if you find yourself in conversation with someone who is depressed, hurt, or frustrated, show them kindness and give them a sympathetic ear; just don't allow yourself to be pulled down too.

We are like actors in a play. The divine will has assigned us our roles in life without consulting us. Some of us will act in a short drama, others in a long one. We might be assigned the part of a poor person, a cripple, a distinguished celebrity or public leader, or an ordinary private citizen.

Although we can't control which roles are assigned to us, it must be our business to act our given role as best as we possibly can and to refrain from complaining about it. Wherever you find yourself and in whatever circumstances, give an impeccable performance.

If you are supposed to be a reader, read; if you are supposed to be a writer, write.

As you think, so you become. Avoid superstitiously investing events with power or meanings they don't have. Keep your head. Our busy minds are forever jumping to conclusions, manufacturing and interpreting signs that aren't there.

Assume, instead, that everything that happens to you does so for some good. That if you decided to be lucky, you are lucky. All events contain an advantage for you — if you look for it!

Freedom is the only worthy goal in life. It is won by disregarding things that lie beyond our control. We cannot have a light heart if our minds are a woeful cauldron of fear and ambition.

Do you wish to be invincible? Then don't enter into combat with what you have no real control over. Your happiness depends on three things, all of which are within your power: your will, your ideas concerning the events in which you are involved, and the use you make of your ideas.

Authentic happiness is always independent of external conditions. Vigilantly practice indifference to external conditions. Your happiness can only be found within.

How easily dazzled and deceived we are by eloquence, job title, degrees, high honors, fancy possessions, expensive clothing, or a suave demeanor. Don't make the mistake of assuming that celebrities, public figures, political leaders, the wealthy, or people with great intellectual or artistic gifts are necessarily happy. To do so is to be bewildered by appearances and will only make you doubt yourself.

Remember: The real essence of good is found only within things under your own control. If you keep this in mind, you won't find yourself feeling falsely envious or forlorn, pitifully comparing yourself and your accomplishments to others.

Stop aspiring to be anyone other than your own best self: for that does fall within your control.

No One Can Hurt You

People don't have the power to hurt you. Even if someone shouts abuse at you or strikes you, if you are insulted, it is always your choice to view what is happening as insulting or not. If someone irritates you, it is only your own response that is irritating you. Therefore, when anyone seems to be provoking you, remember that it is only your judgment of the incident that provokes you. Don't let your emotions get ignited by mere appearances.

Try not to merely react in the moment. Pull back from the situation. Take a wider view; compose yourself.

Spiritual Progress Is Made Through
Confronting Death and Calamity

Instead of averting your eyes from the painful events of life, look at them squarely and contemplate them often. By facing the realities of death, infirmity, loss, and disappointment, you free yourself of illusions and false hopes and you avoid miserable, envious thoughts.

Implant in Yourself
the Ideals You Ought to Cherish

Attach yourself to what is spiritually superior, regardless of what other people think or do. Hold to your true aspirations no matter what is going on around you.

Those who pursue the higher life of wisdom, who seek to live by spiritual principles, must be prepared to be laughed at and condemned.

Many people who have progressively lowered their personal standards in an attempt to win social acceptance and life's comforts bitterly resent those of philosophical bent who refuse to compromise their spiritual ideals and who seek to better themselves. Never live your life in reaction to these diminished souls. Be compassionate toward them, and at the same time hold to what you know is good.

When you begin your program of spiritual progress, chances are the people closest to you will deride you or accuse you of arrogance.

It is your job to comport yourself humbly and to consistently hew to your moral ideals. Cling to what you know in your heart is best. Then, if you are steadfast, the very people who ridiculed you will come to admire you.

If you allow the mean-spirited opinions of others to make you waver in your purpose, you incur a double shame.

Seeking to Please Is a Perilous Trap

In trying to please other people, we find ourselves misdirected toward what lies outside our sphere of influence. In doing so we lose our hold on our life's purpose.

Content yourself with being a lover of wisdom, a seeker of the truth. Return and return again to what is essential and worthy.

Do not try to seem wise to others.

If you want to live a wise life, live it on your own terms and in your own eyes.

Worry and dread are a waste of time and do not set a good example for others. This is especially true regarding your reputation and influence. Why live in fear about things such as whether you will gain public recognition in your profession or community? Or whether you will get the opportunities and perquisites that others do?

Don't be bothered by such concerns as "People don't think well of me," and "I'm a nobody." Even if your reputation were really to matter, you're not responsible for what others think of you. What real difference does it make to your character and well-being if you have a powerful position or get invited to fancy parties? None at all. So how is there any discredit in not being a power broker or a celebrity? And why should you worry about being a nobody when what matters is being a somebody in those areas of your life over which you have control and in which you can make a real difference?

"But without power and repute I won't be able to help my friends," you might say. It's true that you won't give them access to money or the halls of power. But who really expects that such assistance is yours to give and not for others to provide? Who can be expected to give anything that they don't have? "Still, it would be great to have money and power and to be able to share them with my friends." If I can get rich and powerful while preserving my own honor, faithfulness to family, friends, principles, and self-respect, show me how and I'll do it. But if I have to sacrifice my personal integrity, it's stupid and silly to urge me on. Besides, if you had to choose between having a certain amount of money and having a loyal and honorable friend, which would you choose? It's better if you help me become a good person than to push me to do things that threaten my good character.

"Well, what about my obligations to my country?" What do you mean? If you're talking about making grand charitable donations or putting up fancy buildings, is that really an issue? A metalworker doesn't make shoes, and a shoemaker doesn't make weapons. It is enough if everyone does well what he or she is supposed to do. "Well, what if someone else were to do the same thing as me?" That's fine. It doesn't make your contribution any less valuable. "But what about my position in society?" you ask. Whatever position you can hold while preserving your honor and your fidelity to your obligations is fine. But if your desire to contribute to society compromises your moral responsibility, how can you serve your fellow citizens when you've become irresponsible and shameless?

It's better to be a good person and fulfill your obligations than to have renown and power.

Is someone enjoying the privileges, opportunities, or honor you desire? If the advantages that person has secured are good, then delight in that person enjoying them. It is his or her time to prosper. If those advantages actually turn out to be bad, then don't be troubled that they didn't come your way.

Remember: You will never earn the same rewards as others without employing the same methods and investment of time as they do. It is unreasonable to think we can earn rewards without being willing to pay their true price. Those who "win" at something have no real advantage over you, because they had to pay the price for the reward.

It is always our choice whether or not we wish to pay the price for life's rewards. And often it is best for us not to pay the price, for the price might be our integrity. We could be forced to praise someone whom we don't respect.

Learn the will of nature. Study it, pay attention to it, and then make it your own.

The will of nature is revealed to us through everyday experiences common to all people. For example, if a neighbor's child breaks a bowl, or some similar thing, we readily say, "These things happen." When your own bowl breaks, you should respond in the same way as when another person's bowl breaks.

Carry this understanding over to matters of greater emotional import and worldly consequence. Has the child or spouse or other dear one of another person died? Under such circumstances, there is no one who would not say, "Such is the cycle of life. Death happens. Some things are inevitable."

But if our own child or dearly beloved dies, we tend to cry out, "Woe is me! How miserable I am!"

Remember how you feel when you hear the same thing concerning other people. Transfer that feeling to your own current circumstances. Learn to accept events, even death, with intelligence.

Evil does not naturally dwell in the world, in events, or in people. Evil is a by-product of forgetfulness, laziness, or distraction: it arises when we lose sight of our true aim in life.

When we remember that our aim is spiritual progress, we return to striving to be our best selves. This is how happiness is won.

Treasure Your Mind,
Cherish Your Reason, Hold to Your Purpose

Don't surrender your mind.

If someone were to casually give your body away to any old passerby, you would naturally be furious.

Why then do you feel no shame in giving your precious mind over to any person who might wish to influence you? Think twice before you give up your own mind to someone who may revile you, leaving you confused and upset.

Cultivate the habit of surveying and testing a prospective action before undertaking it. Before you proceed, step back and look at the big picture, lest you act rashly on raw impulse. Determine what happens first, consider what that leads to, and then act in accordance with what you've learned.

When we act without circumspection, we might begin a task with great enthusiasm; then, when unforeseen or unwanted consequences follow, we shamefully retreat and are filled with regret: "I would have done this; I could have done that; I should have done it differently."

Suppose you wanted to be victorious at the Olympic Games. That's fine, but fully consider what you're getting yourself into. What does such a desire entail? What needs to happen first? Then what? What will be required of you? And what else follows from that? Is this whole course of action really beneficial to you? If so, carry on.

If you wish to win at the Olympic Games, to prepare yourself properly you would have to follow a strict regimen that stretches you to the limits of your endurance. You would have to submit to demanding rules, follow a suitable diet, vigorously exercise at a regular time in both heat and cold, and give up drinking. You would have to follow the directions of your trainer as if he or she were your doctor. Then, once you are actually in competition, there's a good chance you'd be hurled into a ditch. You might injure your arm, sprain your ankle, get your face slammed in the mud; and after going through all this, you might still be defeated.

After you have contemplated all these possibilities—mindful of all the things that might happen and their consequences—and if your resolve is still strong, then exercise your judgment. If the overall picture still seems beneficial, then do enter the Games—wholeheartedly.

By considering the big picture, you distinguish yourself from the mere dabbler, the person who plays at things as long as they feel comfortable or interesting. This is not noble. Think things through and fully commit! Otherwise, you will be like a child who sometimes pretends he or she is a wrestler, sometimes a soldier, sometimes a musician, sometimes an actor in a tragedy.

Unless we fully give ourselves over to our endeavors, we are hollow, superficial people and we never develop our natural gifts. We've all known people who, like monkeys, mimic whatever seems novel and flashy at the moment. But then their enthusiasm and efforts wane; they drop their projects as soon as they become too familiar or demanding.

A half-hearted spirit has no power. Tentative efforts lead to tentative outcomes. Average people enter into their endeavors headlong and without care. Perhaps they meet with an exemplary figure like Euphrates and become inspired to excel themselves. It is all well and good to do this, but consider first the real nature of your aspirations, and measure that against your capacities.

Be honest with yourself. Clearly assess your strengths and weaknesses. Do you have what it takes to compete at this time? To be a wrestler, for instance, requires extraordinary strength in one's shoulders, back, and thighs. Do you have the physical prowess and agility to be among the best in this sport? It is one thing to wish to be a champion or to do something skillfully; it is another to actually do it and to do it with consummate skill. Different people are made for different things.

Just as certain capacities are required for success in a particular area, so too are certain sacrifices required. If you wish to become proficient in the art of living with wisdom, do you think that you can eat and drink to excess? Do you think you can continue to succumb to anger and your usual habits of frustration and unhappiness? No. If true wisdom is your object and you are sincere, you will have work to do on yourself. You will have to overcome many unhealthy cravings and knee-jerk reactions. You will have to reconsider whom you associate with. Are your friends and associates worthy people? Does their influence—their habits, values, and behavior—elevate you or reinforce the slovenly habits from which you seek escape? The life of wisdom, like anything else, demands its price. You may, in following it, be ridiculed and even end up with the worst of everything in all parts of your public life, including your career, your social standing, and your legal position in the courts.

Once you have given due consideration to all of

the constituent details that compose the effort to live the higher life, venture forth with your utmost effort. Make the necessary sacrifices that are the price for the worthiest of goals: freedom, even-mindedness, and tranquility. If, however, upon honestly appraising your mettle, you are not fit or ready, free yourself from delusion and tread a different, more realistic road.

If you try to be something you're not or strive for something completely beyond your present capacities, you end up as a pathetic dabbler, trying first to be a wise person, then a bureaucrat, then a politician, then a civic leader. These roles are not consistent. You can't be flying off in countless directions, however appealing they are, and at the same time live an integrated, fruitful life.

You can only be one person—either a good person or a bad person. You have two essential choices. Either you can set yourself to developing your reason, cleaving to truth, or you can hanker after externals. The choice is yours and yours alone. You can either put your skills toward internal work or lose yourself to externals, which is to say, be a person of wisdom or follow the common ways of the mediocre.

Our Duties Are Revealed by Our Relations with One Another

You are not an isolated entity, but a unique, irreplaceable part of the cosmos. Don't forget this. You are an essential piece of the puzzle of humanity. Each of us is a part of a vast, intricate, and perfectly ordered human community. But where do you fit into this web of humanity? To whom are you beholden?

Look for and come to understand your connections to other people. We properly locate ourselves within the cosmic scheme by recognizing our natural relations to one another and thereby identifying our duties. Our duties naturally emerge from such fundamental relations as our families, neighborhoods, workplaces, our state or nation. Make it your regular habit to consider your roles—parent, child, neighbor, citizen, leader—and the natural duties that arise from them. Once you know who you are and to whom you are linked, you will know what to do.

If a man is your father, for instance, certain emotional and practical claims follow from this. That he is your father implies a fundamental, durable link between the two of you. You are naturally obligated to care for him, to listen to his advice, to exercise patience in hearing his views, and to respect his guidance.

However, let us suppose that he's not a good father. Perhaps he is fatuous, uneducated, unrefined, or holds views quite different from your own. Does nature give everyone an ideal father, or simply a father? When it comes to your fundamental duty as a son or daughter, whatever your father's character may be, whatever his personality or habits are, is secondary. The divine order does not design people or circumstance according to our tastes. Whether you find him to be agreeable or not, this man is, when all is said and done, your father, and you should live up to all your filial obligations.

Suppose you have a brother or sister who treats you poorly. What difference does that make? There is still a moral imperative to recognize and maintain your fundamental duty to him or her. Focus not on what he or she does, but on keeping to your higher purpose. Your own purpose should seek harmony with nature itself. For this is the true road to freedom. Let others behave as they will — that is not within your control anyway, and thus it's of no concern to you. Understand that nature as a whole is ordered according to reason, but that not everything in nature is reasonable.

When you are faithfully occupied with performing the acts of a wise and decent person, seeking to conform your intentions and acts to the divine will, you do not feel victimized by the words or deeds of others. At worst, those words and deeds will seem amusing or pitiable.

Except for extreme physical abuse, other people cannot hurt you unless you allow them to. And this holds true even if the person is your parent, brother, sister, teacher, or employer. Don't consent to be hurt and you won't be hurt—this is a choice over which you have control.

Most people tend to delude themselves into thinking that freedom comes from doing what feels good or what fosters comfort and ease. The truth is that people who subordinate reason to their feelings of the moment are actually slaves of their desires and aversions. They are ill-prepared to act effectively and nobly when unexpected challenges occur, as they inevitably will.

Authentic freedom places demands on us. In discovering and comprehending our fundamental relations to one another and zestfully performing our duties, true freedom, which all people long for, is indeed possible.

The essence of faithfulness lies first in holding correct opinions and attitudes regarding the Ultimate. Remember that the divine order is intelligent and fundamentally good. Life is not a series of random, meaningless episodes, but an ordered, elegant whole that follows ultimately comprehensible laws.

The divine will exists and directs the universe with justice and goodness. Though it is not always apparent if you merely look at the surface of things, the universe we inhabit is the best possible universe.

Fix your resolve on expecting justice and goodness and order, and they will increasingly reveal themselves to you in all your affairs. Trust that there is a divine intelligence whose intentions direct the universe. Make it your utmost goal to steer your life in accordance with the will of divine order.

When you strive to conform your intentions and actions with the divine order, you don't feel persecuted, helpless, confused, or resentful toward the circumstances of your life. You will feel strong, purposeful, and sure.

Faithfulness is not blind belief; it consists of steadfastly practicing the principle of shunning those things which are not within your control, leaving them to be worked out according to the natural system of responsibilities. Cease trying to anticipate or control events. Instead accept them with grace and intelligence.

It is impossible to remain faithful to your ordained purpose if you drift into imagining that those things outside your power are inherently good or evil. When this happens the habit of blaming outside factors for our lot in life inevitably sets in, and we lose ourselves in a negative spiral of envy, strife, disappointment, anger, and reproach. For by nature all creatures recoil from the things they think would do them harm and seek out and admire those things that seem good and helpful.

The second aspect of faithfulness is the importance of prudently observing the customs of your family, your country, and local community. Perform your community's rituals with a pure heart, without greed or extravagance. In doing so, you join the spiritual order of your people and further the ultimate aspirations of humanity.

Faithfulness is the antidote to bitterness and confusion. It confers the conviction that we are ready for anything the divine will intends for us. Your aim should be to view the world as an integrated whole, to faithfully incline your whole being toward the highest good, and to adopt the will of nature as your own.

When considering the future, remember that all situations unfold as they do regardless of how we feel about them. Our hopes and fears sway us, not events themselves.

Undisciplined people, driven by their personal antipathies and sympathies, are forever on the lookout for signs that build up or reinforce their unexamined views and opinions. Events themselves are impersonal, though judicious people certainly can and should respond to them in beneficial ways.

Instead of personalizing an event ("This is my triumph," "That was his blunder," or "This is my bitter misfortune") and drawing withering conclusions about yourself or human nature, watch for how you can put certain aspects of the event to good use. Is there some less-than-obvious benefit embedded in the event that a trained eye might discern? Pay attention; be a sleuth. Perhaps there is a lesson you can extract and apply to similar events in the future.

In any events, however seemingly dire, there is nothing to prevent us from searching for its hidden opportunity. It is a failure of the imagination not to do so. But to seek out the opportunity in situations requires a great deal of courage, for most people around you will persist in interpreting events in the grossest terms: success or failure, good or bad, right or wrong. These simplistic, polarized categories obscure more creative—and useful—

interpretations of events that are far more advantageous and interesting!

The wise person knows it is fruitless to project hopes and fears on the future. This only leads to forming melodramatic representations in your mind and wasting time.

At the same time, one shouldn't passively acquiesce to the future and what it holds. Simply doing nothing does not avoid risk, but heightens it.

There is a place for prudent planning and for making provision for situations to come. Proper preparation for the future consists of forming good personal habits. This is done by actively pursuing the good in all the particulars of your daily life and by regularly examining your motives to make sure they are free of the shackles of fear, greed, and laziness. If you do this, you won't be buffeted about by outside events.

Train your intentions rather than fooling yourself into thinking you can manipulate outside events. If you are helped by praying or meditating, by all means do so. But seek divine counsel when the application of your own reason hasn't yielded any answers, when you have exhausted other means.

What is a "good" event? What is a "bad" event? There is no such thing! What is a good person? The one who achieves tranquility by having formed the habit of asking on every occasion, "What is the right thing to do now?"

Never Suppress a Generous Impulse

Follow through on all your generous impulses. Do not question them, especially if a friend needs you; act on his or her behalf. Do not hesitate!

Don't sit around speculating about the possible inconvenience, problems, or dangers. As long as you let your reason lead the way, you will be safe.

It is our duty to stand by our friends in their hour of need.

Who exactly do you want to be? What kind of person do you want to be? What are your personal ideals? Whom do you admire? What are their special traits that you would make your own?

It's time to stop being vague. If you wish to be an extraordinary person, if you wish to be wise, then you should explicitly identify the kind of person you aspire to become. If you have a daybook, write down who you're trying to be, so that you can refer to this self-definition. Precisely describe the demeanor you want to adopt so that you may preserve it when you are by yourself or with other people.

Speak Only with Good Purpose

So much attention is given to the moral importance of our deeds and their effects. Those who seek to live the higher life also come to understand the oft-ignored moral power of our words.

One of the clearest marks of the moral life is right speech. Perfecting our speech is one of the keystones of an authentic spiritual program.

First and foremost, think *before* you speak to make sure you are speaking with good purpose. Glib talk disrespects others. Breezy self-disclosure disrespects yourself. So many people feel compelled to give voice to any passing feeling, thought, or impression they have. They randomly dump the contents of their minds without regard to the consequences. This is practically and morally dangerous. If we babble about every idea that occurs to us—big and small—we can easily fritter away in the trivial currents of mindless talk ideas that have true merit. Unchecked speech is like a vehicle wildly lurching out of control and destined for a ditch.

If need be, be mostly silent or speak sparingly. Speech itself is neither good nor evil, but it is so commonly used carelessly that you need to be on your guard. Frivolous talk is hurtful talk; besides, it is unbecoming to be a chatterbox.

Enter into discussions when social or professional occasion calls for it, but be cautious that the spirit and intent of the discussion and its content remain worthy. Prattle is seductive. Stay out of its clutches.

It's not necessary to restrict yourself to lofty subjects or philosophy all the time, but be aware that the common babbling that passes for worthwhile discussion has a corrosive effect on your higher purpose. When we blather about trivial things, we ourselves become trivial, for our attention gets taken up with trivialities. You become what you give your attention to.

We become small-minded if we engage in discussion about other people. In particular, avoid blaming, praising, or comparing people.

Try whenever possible, if you notice the conversation around you decaying into palaver, to see if you can subtly lead the conversation back to more constructive subjects. If, however, you find yourself among indifferent strangers, you can simply remain silent.

Be of good humor and enjoy a good laugh when it is apt, but avoid the kind of unrestrained barroom laughter that easily degenerates into vulgarity or malevolence. Laugh *with*, but never laugh *at*.

If you can, avoid making idle promises whenever possible.

Avoid Most Popular Entertainment

Most of what passes for legitimate entertainment is inferior or foolish and only caters to or exploits people's weaknesses. Avoid being one of the mob who indulges in such pastimes. Your life is too short and you have important things to do. Be discriminating about what images and ideas you permit into your mind. If you yourself don't choose what thoughts and images you expose yourself to, someone else will, and their motives may not be the highest. It is the easiest thing in the world to slide imperceptibly into vulgarity. But there's no need for that to happen if you determine not to waste your time and attention on mindless pap.

Regardless of what others profess, they may not truly live by spiritual values. Be careful whom you associate with. It is human to imitate the habits of those with whom we interact. We inadvertently adopt their interests, their opinions, their values, and their habit of interpreting events. Though many people mean well, they can just the same have a deleterious influence on you because they are undisciplined about what is worthy and what isn't.

Just because some people are nice to you doesn't mean you should spend time with them. Just because they seek you out and are interested in you or your affairs doesn't mean you should associate with them. Be selective about whom you take on as friends, colleagues, and neighbors. All of these people can affect your destiny. The world is full of agreeable and talented folk. The key is to keep company only with people who uplift you, whose presence calls forth your best. But remember that our moral influence is a two-way street, and we should thus make sure by our own thoughts, words, and deeds to be a positive influence on those we deal with. The real test of personal excellence lies in the attention we give to the often neglected small details of our conduct.

Regularly ask yourself, "How are my thoughts, words, and deeds affecting my friends, my spouse, my neighbor, my child, my employer, my subordinates, my fellow citizens? Am I doing my part to contribute to the spiritual progress of all with whom I come in contact?" Make it your business to draw out the best in others by being an exemplar yourself.

Respect your body's needs. Give your body excellent care to promote its health and well-being. Give it everything it absolutely requires, including healthy food and drink, dignified clothing, and a warm and comfortable home. Do not, however, use your body as an occasion for show or luxury.

Avoid Casual Sex

Abstain from casual sex and particularly avoid sexual intercourse before you get married. This may sound prudish or old-fashioned, but it is a time-tested way by which we demonstrate respect for ourselves and others. Sex is not a game. It gives rise to very real enduring emotional and practical consequences. To ignore this is to debase yourself, and to disregard the significance of human relationships.

If, however, you know someone who has had casual sex, don't self-righteously try to win them over to your own views.

An active sex life within a framework of personal commitment augments the integrity of the people involved and is part of a flourishing life.

Don't be afraid of verbal abuse or criticism.

Only the morally weak feel compelled to defend or explain themselves to others. Let the quality of your deeds speak on your behalf. We can't control the impressions others form about us, and the effort to do so only debases our character.

So, if anyone should tell you that a particular person has spoken critically of you, don't bother with excuses or defenses. Just smile and reply, "I guess that person doesn't know about all my other faults. Otherwise, he wouldn't have mentioned only these."

Conduct Yourself with Dignity

No matter where you find yourself, comport yourself as if you were a distinguished person.

While the behavior of many people is dictated by what is going on around them, hold yourself to a higher standard. Take care to avoid parties or games where thoughtless revelry and carousing are the norm. If you find yourself at a public event, remain rooted in your own purposes and ideals.

Emulate Worthy Role Models

One of the best ways to elevate your character immediately is to find worthy role models to emulate. If you have the opportunity to meet with an important person, don't be nervous. Invoke the characteristics of the people you admire most and adopt their manners, speech, and behavior as your own. There is nothing false in this. We all carry the seeds of greatness within us, but we need an image as a point of focus in order that they may sprout.

At the same time, just because you are meeting a person of great merit doesn't mean you should be overly awed. People are just people, regardless of their talent or influence.

Exercise Discretion When Conversing

Self-importance is not the way of the true philosopher. Nobody enjoys the company of a braggart. Don't oppress people with dramatic stories of your own exploits. Nobody cares that much about your war stories and dramatic adventures, though they might indulge you for a while to appear polite. To speak frequently and excessively of your own achievements is tiresome and pompous.

You don't need to be the class clown. Nor do you need to resort to other indelicate methods in order to convince others you are clever, sophisticated, or affable.

Aggressive, glib, or showy talk should be completely avoided. It just lowers you in the esteem of your acquaintances.

Many people casually pepper their speech with obscenities in an attempt to bring force and intensity to their speech or to embarrass others. Refuse to go along with such talk. When people around you start to slip into indecent, pointless speech, leave if you can, or at least be silent and let your look of seriousness show that you are offended by such coarse talk.

Let your reason be supreme.

Inculcate the habit of deliberation.

Practice the art of testing whether particular things are actually good or not. Learn to wait and assess instead of always reacting from untrained instinct. Spontaneity is not a virtue in and of itself.

If some pleasure is promised to you and it seductively calls to you, step back and give yourself some time before mindlessly jumping at it. Dispassionately turn the matter over in your mind: Will this pleasure bring but a momentary delight, or real, lasting satisfaction? It makes a difference in the quality of our life and the kind of person we become when we learn how to distinguish between cheap thrills and meaningful, lasting rewards.

If, in calmly considering this pleasure, you realize that if you indulge in it you will regret it, abstain and rejoice in your forbearance. Reinforce the triumph of your character and you will be strengthened.

Take a Stand

Once you have deliberated and determined that a course of action is wise, never discredit your judgment. Stand squarely behind your decision. Chances are there may indeed be people who misunderstand your intentions and who may even condemn you. But if, according to your best judgment, you are acting rightly, you have nothing to fear. Take a stand. Don't be cravenly noncommittal.

Propriety and logic are different things, and each has its appropriate application.

The proposition "Either it is day or it is night" works well in a disjunctive argument, but not as well in a friendly conversation. Likewise, at a banquet it may make sense to take the largest share of food if you are really hungry, but it would be bad manners to do so.

When you dine with others, be aware not only how much your body appreciates the delicacies offered, but also how important good manners and personal refinement are.

Self-Mastery Depends on Self-Honesty

Know first who you are and what you're capable of. Just as nothing great is created instantly, the same goes for the perfecting of our talents and aptitudes. We are always learning, always growing. It is right to accept challenges. This is how we progress to the next level of intellectual, physical, or moral development. Still, don't kid yourself: If you try to be something or someone you are not, you belittle your true self and end up not developing in those areas that you would have excelled at quite naturally.

Within the divine order, we each have our own special calling. Listen to yours and follow it faithfully.

Just as when you walk you are careful not to step on a nail or injure your foot, you should similarly take the utmost care not to in any way impair the highest faculty of your mind. The virtuous life depends on reason first and foremost. If you safeguard your reason, it will safeguard you.

Through vigilance, we can forestall the tendency to excess. Your possessions should be proportionate to the needs of your body, just as the shoe should fit the foot.

Without moral training, we can be induced to excess. In the case of shoes, for instance, many people are tempted to buy fancy, exotic shoes when all that is needed is comfortable, well-fitting, durable footwear.

Once we fall, however slightly, into immoderation, momentum gathers and we can be lost to whim.

Females are especially burdened by the attention they receive for their pleasing appearance. From the time they are young, they are flattered by males or evaluated only in terms of their outward appearance.

Unfortunately, this can make a woman feel suited only to give men pleasure, and her true inner gifts sadly atrophy. She may feel compelled to put great effort and time into enhancing her outer beauty and distorting her natural self to please others.

Sadly, many people—both men and women—place all their emphasis on managing their physical appearance and the impression they make on others.

Those who seek wisdom come to understand that even though the world may reward us for wrong or superficial reasons, such as our physical appearance, the family we come from, and so on, what really matters is who we are inside and who we are becoming.

Care About Your Mind More Than Your Body

Those who are morally untrained spend an inordinate amount of time on their bodies. Carry out your animal functions incidentally. Your main attention should be given to the care and development of your reason. For through your reason, you are able to understand nature's laws.

If people treat you disrespectfully or speak un-
kindly about you, remember that they do so from
their impression that it is right to do so.

It is unrealistic to expect people to see you as
you see yourself. If people reach conclusions based
on false impressions, they are the ones hurt rather
than you, because it is they who are misguided.
When someone interprets a true proposition as a
false one, the proposition itself isn't hurt; only the
person who holds the wrong view is deceived, and
thus damaged. Once you clearly understand this,
you will be less likely to feel affronted by others,
even if they revile you. You can say to yourself, "It
seemed so to that person, but that is only his impression."

Everything has two handles: one by which it may be carried, the other by which it can't.

If, for example, your brother or sister treats you poorly, don't grasp the situation by the handle of hurt or injustice, or you won't be able to bear it and you will become bitter. Do the opposite. Grasp the situation by the handle of familial ties. In other words, focus on the fact that this is your brother or sister, that you were brought up together, and thus have an enduring, unbreakable bond. Viewing the situation that way, you understand it correctly and preserve your equilibrium.

The life of wisdom is a life of reason. It is important to learn how to think clearly. Clear thinking is not a haphazard enterprise. It requires proper training. It is through clear thinking that we are able to properly direct our will, stick with our true purpose, and discover the connections we have to others and the duties that follow from those relationships. Every person should learn how to identify mushy and fallacious thinking. Study how inferences are legitimately derived, so that you avoid drawing unfounded conclusions.

For instance, note the following examples of faulty logic: "I am richer than you; therefore, I am better than you." One encounters such absurd assertions as this all the time, but they are completely fallacious. The valid inference that can be drawn is this: "I am richer than you; therefore I have more possessions or money than you do."

Another example: "I speak more persuasively than you; therefore, I am better than you." From this we can only conclude, "I speak more persuasively than you; therefore my speech carries more effect than yours."

But remember: Your character is independent of property or persuasive speech.

Take the time to assiduously study clear thinking and you won't be hoodwinked. Strong education in logic and the rules of effective argument will serve you well.

When we name things correctly, we comprehend them correctly, without adding information or judgments that aren't there. Does someone bathe quickly? Don't say he bathes poorly, but quickly. Name the situation as it is; don't filter it through your judgments.

Does someone drink a lot of wine? Don't say she is a drunk but that she drinks a lot. Unless you possess a comprehensive understanding of her life, how do you know if she is a drunk?

Do not risk being beguiled by appearances and constructing theories and interpretations based on distortions through misnaming. Give your assent only to what is actually true.

Wisdom Is Revealed Through Action, Not Talk

Don't declare yourself to be a wise person or discuss your spiritual aspirations with people who won't appreciate them. Show your character and your commitment to personal nobility through your actions.

Don't be puffed up with pride if you are able to provide for your needs with very little cost. The first task of the person who wishes to live wisely is to free himself or herself from the confines of self-absorption.

Consider how much more frugal the poor are than we, how much better they forebear hardship. If you want to develop your ability to live simply, do it for yourself, do it quietly, and don't do it to impress others.

Most people don't realize that both help and harm come from within ourselves. Instead they look to externals, mesmerized by appearances.

Wise people, on the other hand, realize that we are the source of everything good or bad for us. They therefore don't resort to blaming and accusing others. They aren't driven to convince people they are worthy or special or distinguished.

If wise people experience challenges, they look to themselves; if they are commended by others, they quietly smile to themselves, unmoved; if they are slandered, they don't feel the need to defend their name.

But they go about their actions with vigilance, assuming that all is well, yet not perfectly secure. They harmonize their desires with life as it is, and seek to avoid only the things that would prevent their ability to exercise their will properly. They exercise moderation in all their affairs. And if they seem ignorant or unsophisticated, it is of no concern to them. They know that they only have to watch out for themselves and the direction of their own desires.

If someone tries to impress you, claiming to understand the writings and ideas of a great thinker such as Chrysippus, think to yourself, the important thing is not to be able merely to speak fluently about abstruse subjects. What is essential is to understand nature and align your intentions and actions with the way things are. The person who truly understands Chrysippus's writings or the precepts of any great mind is the person who actually applies the philosopher's teachings. There is a big difference between saying valuable things and doing valuable things.

Don't give too much weight to erudition alone. Look to the example of people whose actions are consistent with their professed principles.

Practicing Principles
Matters More Than Proving Them

The life of wisdom begins with learning how to put principles, such as "We ought not to lie," into practice. The second step is to demonstrate the truth of the principles, such as why it is that we ought not to lie. The third step, which connects the first two, is to indicate why the explanations suffice to justify the principles. While the second and third steps are valuable, it is the first step that matters most. For it is all too easy and common to lie while cleverly demonstrating that lying is wrong.

Now is the time to get serious about living your ideals. Once you have determined the spiritual principles you wish to exemplify, abide by these rules as if they were laws, as if it were indeed sinful to compromise them.

Don't mind if others don't share your convictions. How long can you afford to put off who you really want to be? Your nobler self cannot wait any longer.

Put your principles into practice—now. Stop the excuses and the procrastination. This is your life! You aren't a child anymore. The sooner you set yourself to your spiritual program, the happier you will be. The longer you wait, the more you will be vulnerable to mediocrity and feel filled with shame and regret, because you know you are capable of better.

From this instant on, vow to stop disappointing yourself. Separate yourself from the mob. Decide to be extraordinary and do what you need to do—now.

Essential Teachings
on Virtue, Happiness, and Tranquility

The Stoic conception of virtue espoused by Epictetus has left an indelible and underappreciated imprint on our culture. Descartes, Spinoza, Rousseau, Nietzsche, Marx, and the Founding Fathers of the United States are just a few of the movers and shakers who owe a great debt to Stoic ethical thought.

Virtue, until its very recent revival, has sounded old-fashioned or even prissy to our modern ears. Epictetus's teachings on virtue had nothing to do with being a goody-goody or a doormat. Virtue, happiness, and tranquility are not separate or distinct experiences but co-emergent states.

While he advocated being good for its own sake, his practical observation was that a virtuous life leads to inner coherence and outward harmony. There is great relief in being morally consistent: The soul relaxes, and we can thus efficiently move forward in our endeavors, as Epictetus would say, "without hindrance."

Inner confusion and evil itself spring from ambiguity. Epictetus coaches us to call forth the best we have by making our personal moral code explicit to ourselves. Freedom, ease, and confidence are won as our outward actions gradually conform to this code. He asks us to minimize the importance we would place on "external" choices, what we might today call "lifestyle choices," and to concentrate on the small but significant inner moral choices we make in the course of any day.

Philosophy's main task is to respond to the soul's cry; to make sense of and thereby free ourselves from the hold of our griefs and fears.

Philosophy calls us when we've reached the end of our rope. The insistent feeling that something is not right with our lives and the longing to be restored to our better selves will not go away. Our fears of death and being alone, our confusion about love and sex, and our sense of impotence in the face of our anger and outsized ambitions bring us to ask our first sincere philosophical questions.

It's true: there is no *obviously* apparent meaning to our lives. Cruelty, injustice, bodily discomfort, illness, annoyances, and inconveniences big and small are the prosaic facts of any day. So what do we do about this? How do we—in spite of the pain and suffering in the outside world and our own wayward emotions—live ennobled lives rather than succumbing to a despairing numbness and merely coping like a mule with tedium and unbidden responsibilities?

When the soul cries out, it is a sign that we have arrived at a necessary, mature stage of self-reflection. The secret is not to get stuck there dithering or wringing your hands, but to move forward by resolving to heal *yourself*. Philosophy asks us to move into courage. Its remedy is the unblinking excavation of the faulty and specious premises on which we base our lives and our personal identity.

The Real Purpose of Philosophy

True philosophy doesn't involve exotic rituals, mysterious liturgy, or quaint beliefs. Nor is it just abstract theorizing and analysis. It is, of course, the love of wisdom. It is the art of living a good life. As such, it must be rescued from religious gurus and from professional philosophers lest it be exploited as an esoteric cult or as a set of detached intellectual techniques or brain teasers to show how clever you are. Philosophy is intended for everyone, and it is authentically practiced only by those who wed it with action in the world toward a better life for all.

Philosophy's purpose is to illuminate the ways our soul has been infected by unsound beliefs, untrained tumultuous desires, and dubious life choices and preferences that are unworthy of us. Self-scrutiny applied with kindness is the main antidote. Besides rooting out the soul's corruptions, the life of wisdom is also meant to stir us from our lassitude and move us in the direction of an energetic, cheerful life.

Skilled use of logic, disputation, and the developed ability to name things correctly are some of the instruments philosophy gives us to achieve abiding clear-sightedness and inner tranquility, which is true happiness.

This happiness, which is our aim, must be correctly understood. Happiness is commonly mistaken for passively experienced pleasure or leisure. That conception of happiness is good only as far as it goes. The only worthy object of all our efforts is a flourishing life.

True happiness is a verb. It's the ongoing dynamic performance of worthy deeds. The flourishing life, whose foundation is virtuous intention, is something we continually improvise, and in doing so our souls mature. Our life has usefulness to ourselves and to the people we touch.

We become philosophers to discover what is really true and what is merely the accidental result of flawed reasoning, recklessly acquired erroneous judgments, well-intentioned but misguided teachings of parents and teachers, and unexamined acculturation.

To ease our soul's suffering, we engage in disciplined introspection in which we conduct thought-experiments to strengthen our ability to distinguish between wholesome and lazy, hurtful beliefs and habits.

The first step to living wisely is to relinquish self-conceit.

See the delusional folly in being a nervous know-it-all whose giddy mind is always prattling on about its knee-jerk impressions of events and other people, forcing current experiences into previously formed categories: "Oh yes, this thing here is just like such and such."

Behold the world fresh—as it is, on its own terms—through the eyes of a beginner. To know that you do *not* know and to be willing to admit that you do not know without sheepishly apologizing is real strength and sets the stage for learning and progress in any endeavor.

The wisest among us appreciate the natural limits of our knowledge and have the mettle to preserve their naiveté. They understand how little all of us really know about anything. There is no such thing as conclusive, once-and-for-all knowledge. The wise do not confuse information or data, however prodigious or cleverly deployed, with comprehensive knowledge or transcendent wisdom. They say things like "Hmmm" or "Is that so!" a lot. Once you realize how little we do know, you are not so easily duped by fast-talkers, splashy gladhanders, and demagogues. Spirited curiosity is an emblem of the flourishing life.

Arrogance is the banal mask for cowardice; but far more important, it is the most potent impediment to the flourishing life. Clear thinking and self-importance cannot logically coexist. Humanity has no inherent pecking order, despite outward appearances. *Everyone* in this world is important. If you really want peace of mind and success in your endeavors, forego self-importance.

Conceit is an iron gate that admits no new knowledge, no expansive possibilities, nor constructive ideas. Indulging in excessive pride in your own knowledge, abilities, or experiences and attempting to take on more power or authority than is your due is fatal. Such preening not only alienates others, since an overbearing lout is suffocating to be around, but also leads to complacency, precluding change in a wholesome direction. You keep running around in the same familiar circles; you get caught in the same sticky webs. Nothing novel or festive ever happens.

Stop jabbering like a magpie. Notice what's *actually* happening, not just what you *think* is happening or *wish* were happening. Look and Listen.

To do anything well you must have the humility to bumble around a bit, to follow your nose, to get lost, to goof. Have the courage to try an undertaking and possibly do it poorly. Unremarkable lives are marked by the fear of not looking capable when trying something new.

New experiences are meant to deepen our lives and advance us to new levels of competence; they are not meant to be used by the self-important as fodder for shoring up their previously adopted views and conclusions.

Important knowledge and personal guidance dwell in unexpected places. If you wish to see them and avail yourself of them when you come upon them, then guard yourself lest you become vainglorious and uncritically smug.

The legitimate glow of satisfaction at accomplishing a hard-won *worthy* goal should not be confused with arrogance, which is characterized by self-preoccupation and lack of interest in the feelings or affairs of others.

The flourishing life is not achieved by techniques. You can't trick yourself into a life well-lived. Neither is it achieved by following five easy steps or some charismatic figure's dogma. A flourishing life depends on our responding, as best we can, to those things uniquely incumbent on us.

To live an extraordinary life means we must elevate our moral stature by culturing our character. The untrained brood about the constituent elements of their lives. They waste precious time in regret or wishing their particulars were different ("If only I lived in a better house or town, had a different spouse, a more glamorous job, more time to myself ..."). The morally trained, rather than resenting or dodging their current life situations and duties, give thanks for them and fully immerse themselves in their duties to their family, friends, neighbors, and job. When we succumb to whining, we diminish our possibilities.

The overvaluation of money, status, and competition poisons our personal relations. The flourishing life cannot be achieved until we moderate our desires and see how superficial and fleeting they are.

The *first* steps toward wisdom are the most strenuous, because our weak and stubborn souls dread exertion (without absolute guarantee of reward) and the unfamiliar. As you progress in your efforts, your resolve is fortified and self-improvement progressively comes easier. By and by it actually becomes difficult to work counter to your own best interest.

By the steady but patient commitment to removing unsound beliefs from our souls, we become increasingly adept at seeing through our flimsy fears, our bewilderment in love, and our lack of self control. We stop trying to look good to others. One day, we contentedly realize we've stopped playing to the crowd.

Good Is Good

Goodness exists independently of our conception of it. The good is out there and it always has been out there, even before we began to exist.

Be suspicious of convention.

Take charge of your own thinking.

Rouse yourself from the daze of unexamined habit.

Popular perceptions, values, and ways of doing things are rarely the wisest. Many pervasive beliefs would not pass appropriate tests of rationality. Conventional thinking—its means and ends—is essentially uncreative and uninteresting. Its job is to preserve the status quo for overly self-defended individuals and institutions.

On the other hand, there is no inherent virtue in *new* ideas. Judge ideas and opportunities on the basis of whether they are life-giving. Give your assent to that which promotes humaneness, justice, beneficial growth, kindness, possibility, and benefit to the human community.

Examine things as they appear to your own mind; objectively consider what is said by others, and then establish your own convictions.

Socially taught beliefs are frequently unreliable. So many of our beliefs have been acquired through accident and irresponsible or ignorant teaching. Many of these beliefs are so deeply ingrained that they are hidden from our own view. The commonplace sluggishness of the lives lived by the undisciplined is dangerously contagious, for we are often exposed to no alternative healthful way of living. Awaken and be vigilant. Take stock of your habits to preserve your higher standards.

Many people declare with all sincerity that they are committed to their own integrity, while engaging in thoughtless or intemperate actions. They proceed willy-nilly, undercutting their otherwise well-intentioned efforts by failing to face themselves and to articulate a coherent personal moral code to which their future actions would conform. Don't listen to what people *say*. Watch what they *do* and evaluate the attendant consequences.

Just as we must clean, order, and maintain our homes to move forward with anything; we need to do the same with our minds. For not only do we risk inefficiency by failing to do so, we invite our soul's very corruption. A disorganized, foggy soul is dangerous, for it is vulnerable to the influence of better organized but unsavory influences.

Trust nothing and nobody but yourself. Be ceaselessly watchful over your beliefs and impulses.

The difference between the instructed and the ignorant is that the wise know that the virtuous are invincible. They aren't tricked and provoked by the way things *appear* to be.

The instructed respect the kinship we share with the Ultimate and thus comport themselves as a compassionate, self-aware citizen of the universe. They understand that the wise life, which leads to tranquility, comes from conforming to Nature and to Reason.

Be a Citizen of the World

One cannot pursue one's own highest good without at the same time necessarily promoting the good of others. A life based on narrow self-interest cannot be esteemed by any honorable measurement. Seeking the very best in ourselves means actively caring for the welfare of other human beings. Our human contract is not with the few people with whom our affairs are most immediately intertwined, nor to the prominent, rich, or well educated, but to all our human brethren.

View yourself as a citizen of a worldwide community and act accordingly.

Consider your deepest and most secret yearnings as if they were merely facts, so you can see how insubstantial and hysterical they are. There is no shame in pursuing worldly success: It's normal. Your trouble lies not in the pursuit itself, but *how* you pursue it. You allow your frenzied, misguided desires and fears to color your judgment. So you overevaluate the intrinsic worth of your pursuits. You bank on your pursuits to give you happiness, thus confusing means with ends.

Understand that while the pursuit of such indifferent objectives is natural, neither failure nor success in attaining them has the slightest bearing on your happiness.

Don't just say you have read books. Show that through them you have learned to think better, to be a more discriminating and reflective person. Books are the training weights of the mind. They are very helpful, but it would be a bad mistake to suppose that one has made progress simply by having internalized their contents.

One of two things will happen when you socialize with others. You either become like your companions, or you bring them over to your own ways. Just as when a dead coal contacts a live one, either the first will extinguish the last, or the last kindle the first. Great is the danger; so be circumspect on entering into personal associations, even and especially light-hearted ones.

Most of us do not possess sufficiently developed steadfastness to steer our companions to our own purpose, so we end up being carried along by the crowd. Our own values and ideals become fuzzy and tainted; our resolve is destabilized.

It's hard to resist when friends or associates start speaking brashly. Caught off guard when our associates broach ignoble subjects, we are swept along by the social momentum. It is the nature of conversation that its multiple meanings, innuendoes, and personal motivations move along at such a fast clip they can instantly shift in unwholesome directions, sullying everyone involved. So until wise sentiments are fixed into you as if they were instinct and you have thus acquired some power of self-defense, choose your associations with care and monitor the thrust of the conversations in which you find yourself.

Generally, we're all doing the best we can.

When someone speaks to you curtly, disregards what you say, performs what seems to be a thought-less gesture or even an outright evil act, think to yourself, "If I were that person and had endured the same trials, borne the same heartbreaks, had the same parents, and so on, I probably would have done or said the same thing." We are not privy to the stories behind people's actions, so we should be patient with others and suspend our judgment of them, recognizing the limits of our understanding. This does not mean we condone evil deeds or en-dorse the idea that different actions carry the same moral weight.

When people do not act as you would wish them to, exercise the muscles of your good nature by shrugging your shoulders and saying to yourself "Oh well." Then let the incident go.

Try, also, to be as kind to *yourself* as possible. Do not measure yourself against others or even against your ideal self. Human betterment is a gradual, two-steps-forward, one-step-back effort.

Forgive others for their misdeeds over and over again. This gesture fosters inner ease.

Forgive yourself over and over and over again. Then try to do better next time.

The Virtuous Are Consistent

To live a life of virtue, you have to become consistent, even when it isn't convenient, comfortable, or easy.

It is incumbent that your thoughts, words, and deeds match up. This is a higher standard than that held by the mob. Most people want to be good and try somewhat to be good, but then a moral challenge presents itself and lassitude sets in.

When your thoughts, words, and deeds form a seamless fabric, you streamline your efforts and thus eliminate worry and dread. In this way, it is *easier* to seek goodness than to conduct yourself in a haphazard fashion or according to the feelings of the moment.

When you free yourself of the distractions of shallow or illusory pleasures and devote yourself instead to your rightful duties, you can relax. When you know you've done the best you can under the circumstances, you can have a light heart. Your mind doesn't have to moonlight, making excuses, thinking up alibis, defending your honor, feeling guilty or remorseful. You can simply, cleanly, move on to the next thing.

It's so simple really: If you say you're going to do something, do it. If you start something, finish it.

We are born into essential goodness, endowed with natural intuitions about what is good and worthy and what is not. This endemic moral capacity must then be trained deliberately and systematically to bring out its best in full maturity.

It is natural to want to be well-regarded by others, but you must gradually wean yourself from such dependence on the admiration or honor given or withheld by others. In good fortune or adversity, it is the good will with which you perform deeds that matters—not the outcome. So take your attention off of what you think other people think and off of the results of your actions. Defer instead to your original moral intuitions and follow them.

The untrained response to robbers and thugs and to those who otherwise err is outrage and retribution. Wrongdoers need to be rightly understood to form the correct response to their behavior.

The appropriate response to bad deeds is pity for the perpetrators, since they have adopted unsound beliefs and are deprived of the most valuable human capacity: the ability to differentiate between what's truly good and bad for them. Their original moral intuitions have been distorted, so they have no chance at inner serenity.

Whenever someone does something foolish, pity him rather than yield to hatred and anger as so many do.

We are only enraged at the foolish because we make idols of those things which such people take from us.

Virtue is our aim and purpose. The virtue that leads to enduring happiness is not a *quid pro quo* goodness. (I'll be good "in order to" get something.) Goodness in and of itself *is* the practice *and* the reward.

Goodness isn't ostentatious piety or showy good manners. It's a lifelong series of subtle readjustments of our character. We fine-tune our thoughts, words, and deeds in a progressively wholesome direction. The virtue inheres in our intentions and our deeds, not in the results.

Why should we bother being good? To be good is to be happy; to be tranquil and worry-free. When you actively engage in gradually refining yourself, you retreat from your lazy ways of covering yourself or making excuses. Instead of feeling a persistent current of low-level shame, you move forward by using the creative possibilities of *this* moment, your current situation. You begin to fully inhabit this moment, instead of seeking escape or wishing that what is going on were otherwise. You move *through* your life by being thoroughly *in* it.

The virtuous life holds these as treasures: your own right action, your fidelity, honor, and decency.

Virtue is not a matter of degree, but an absolute.

Pursue the good ardently. But if your efforts fall short, accept the result and move on.

What Is Important and What Isn't

This is our predicament: Over and over again, we lose sight of what is important and what isn't.

We crave things over which we have no control, and are not satisfied by the things within our control.

We need to regularly stop and take stock; to sit down and determine within ourselves which things are worth valuing and which things are not; which risks are worth the cost and which are not. Even the most confusing or hurtful aspects of life can be made more tolerable by clear seeing and by choice.

Rationality isn't everything. There are many domains of life to which it lacks access. The greatest mysteries of existence exceed its reach. Still our reason is the best faculty we have to safeguard our integrity.

Most people do not understand the correct use of arguments by inference and the proper use of logical forms, so they conduct themselves in a random, overly reactive, or muddled fashion and are easily misled.

Clear thinking is not a bloodless art. Reason's job is to critically test our conjectures, both our interpretations and our method of arriving at them. Reason is not an end but an indispensable instrument.

Questions are the engines of reason. Thus you need to learn how to frame questions sensibly, rather than emotionally. If your ability to think clearly is compromised, your moral life can become fuzzy and equivocal.

Reason can distinguish error from truth and a deep truth from a petty one. The marks of good reasoning are clarity, consistency, rigor, precision of definitions, and avoidance of ambiguity.

Hasten to your training in clear thinking so you can confidently enter a complex argument and not be thrown by it.

Your relentless *pursuit* of wisdom postpones your actually possessing it. Quit chasing after tonics and new teachers. The latest fashionable sage or book or diet or belief doesn't move you in the direction of a flourishing life. You do. Renounce externals once and for all.

Practice self-sufficiency. Don't remain a dependent, malleable patient: Become your own soul's doctor.

Regardless of what is going on around you, make the best of what is in your power, and take the rest as it occurs.

Practice having a grateful attitude and you will be happy. If you take a broad view of what befalls each person and appreciate the usefulness of things that happen, it is natural to give thanks to the Ultimate for everything that happens in the world.

Take care not to casually discuss matters that are of great importance to you with people who are not important to you. Your affairs will become drained of preciousness. You undercut your own purposes when you do this. This is especially dangerous when you are in the early stages of an undertaking.

Other people feast like vultures on our ideas. They take it upon themselves to blithely interpret, judge, and twist what matters most to you, and your heart sinks. Let your ideas and plans incubate before you parade them in front of the naysayers and trivializers.

Most people only know how to respond to an idea by pouncing on its shortfalls rather than identifying its potential merits. Practice self-containment so that your enthusiasm won't be frittered away.

All human beings seek the happy life, but many confuse the means—for example, wealth and status—with that life itself. This misguided focus on the means to a good life makes people get further from the happy life. The really worthwhile things are the virtuous activities that make up the happy life, not the external means that may seem to produce it.

Every habit and faculty is preserved and increased by its corresponding actions: The habit of walking makes us better walkers, regular running makes us better runners. It is the same regarding matters of the soul. Whenever you are angry, you increase your anger; you have increased a habit and added fuel to a fire.

If you don't want an angry temper, then don't feed the habit. Give it nothing to help its increase. Be quiet at first and reckon the days in which you have not been angry. "I used to be angry every day; now every other day; then every third and fourth day." As time goes on, the habit is first weakened and is then eventually overridden by a wiser response.

Caretake *this* moment.

Immerse yourself in its particulars. Respond to *this* person, *this* challenge, *this* deed.

Quit the evasions. Stop giving yourself needless trouble.

It is time to really live; to fully inhabit the situation you happen to be in now. You are not some disinterested bystander. Participate. Exert yourself.

Respect your partnership with providence. Ask yourself often, How may I perform this particular deed such that it would be consistent with and acceptable to the divine will? Heed the answer and get to work.

When your doors are shut and your room is dark, you are not alone. The will of nature is within you as your natural genius is within. Listen to its importunings. Follow its directives.

As concerns the art of living, the material is your own life. No great thing is created suddenly. There must be time.

Give your best and always be kind.

Plus:

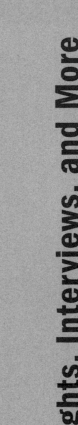

Plus: **Insights, Interviews, and More**

Epi-Who?
How a 2000-Year-Old Dead White Male Changed My Life

Sharon Lebell

By happy accident, I—a harried mother of four children and two stepchildren, as well as a sometime musician living in a small town in northern California circa the third millennium—became the improbable mouthpiece for an all-but-forgotten ancient Western sage named Epictetus, who was born a slave in the eastern outreaches of the Roman Empire in 55 AD.

I make my living writing inspirational books, and in the mid-1990s, an editor at my publisher, HarperSanFrancisco, had what turned out to be a stunningly prescient hunch. He predicted that the then widespread baby-boomer fascination with "right-brainy," enlightenment-oriented Eastern religions—particularly Buddhism—might soon give way to a renewed appreciation of our "left-brainy," morality-based *Western* philosophical tradition's treasure trove of life wisdom.

Anticipating this spiritual backlash, he asked if I would write a contemporary interpretation (*not* a translation!) of Epictetus's most important teachings in the spirit of Stephen Mitchell's easy-to-read version of the *Tao Te Ching*.

Whoa! Epi-who? Surely, you must mean Epicurus, right? The pleasure guy?

Like most people whose classically bereft education didn't happen to include a Talmudic-style perusal of Stoic philosophy, of whom Epictetus is a seminal exponent, I had to do some frantic homework to find out who in God's name this dead, white classical guy was.

It turns out Epictetus (pronounced "Eh-pick-tee-tis") was one of the wisest teachers, Eastern or Western, who ever lived. He formulated a way of life that leads to enduring happiness, peace of mind, and outward personal effectiveness. As I submerged myself in this overlooked philosopher's two surviving documents, the *Enchiridion* and the *Discourses*, I gradually became won over by his inspiring noble philosophy. At first I was skeptical of, for example, Epictetus's emphasis on duty and decorum, which seemed, at first blush, quaint and rigid to someone of my generation. And his repeated exhortation to understand and distinguish between that which you can control and that which you can't rubbed up against my seemingly irrepressible desire to influence outcomes. The more closely I read Epictetus and really listened to what he was saying, the more I realized that Epictetus was offering up a very workable and perennial approach to dealing with adversity, fear, and grief. His was a philosophy of personal ennoblement, resilience, kindness, and even quietly confident joy. Well, who wouldn't want some of that?

But who did I think I was trying to convey the essential wisdom of a two-millennia-old Greek philosopher? I wasn't a credentialed member of a university philosophy or classics faculty. Academics love to denigrate mere popularizers. I wasn't old, fusty, bearded, or wise, and I wasn't, well, a guy. I didn't read Greek, and I didn't cotton to athletic and military metaphors the way guys, including Epictetus, do, whether they happen to be venerable ancient sages or your average yahoo holding forth in a sports bar. And like most people, I also didn't have a lot of time to sit around chewing the fat about philosophy.

But none of this matters. The beauty of Epictetus's philosophy is that he doesn't particularly care *what* your life circumstances are. You can be a future Roman emperor, like Marcus Aurelius, Epictetus's most famous student; you can be a lame, former slave like Epictetus himself; or you can be a California mother with a propensity for melodrama, whose house looks like a hurricane whipped through it most days. Epictetus's philosophy speaks to *anyone* who has hassles, longings, problems, soul-withering sorrows, vanities, outsized ambition, and one hopes, visitations of ineffable joy, moments of sweet triumph, and marvelous wind-at-your-back sorts of days. Epictetus is for all of us.

What I've got, which is probably what you've got, is a whole bunch of personal life circumstances: problems to solve; opportunities to recognize and seize; people to love right and to, ideally, not hurt; moments to appreciate; talents to cultivate; knowledge to acquire; perhaps kids to wrangle; and teeth to brush. And, if you are like me, a *regular* person and an exceedingly imperfect person at that—not a spiritual professional: monk, saint, bodhisattva, avatar, tulku, priest, prophet, or spiritual know-it-all on the circuit teaching teleseminars and promoting your Web site—Epictetus's Stoicism will have quite a bit to say to you, because Stoicism is a philosophy of *real life* for *real people* living *real lives.*

It's a philosophy for people who make mistakes and harbor regrets. It's also a philosophy for grown-ups. Stoicism asks you to quit mewling and making excuses and to face this problem you have, which is that your life is life-ing away from you right now and you have to figure out what you're going to do about it. Epictetus wags his sagacious finger at you and says: "I know you're a very busy person, so let's not focus on labor-intensive, long-term, and possibly elusive efforts like trying to get enlightened or achieving rapturous mystical states. We're gonna keep it simple and real here. Let's shoot for making the most meaningful life possible within the particular personal life circumstances you find yourself in right now. Let's get on with the task of becoming your best possible self." (He means by degrees, mind you, not in one fell swoop. Epictetus is as realistic about human potential and motivation as he is humanistically compassionate.) I think it is reasonable to assume that if Epictetus were alive today, his quintessential exhortation to us all would be something along the lines of: "Let's quit trying to be mystics or saints, and instead try our utmost to be mensches (fully honorable, decent people)."

One of the unexpected bonuses of interpreting Epictetus is discovering that I'm part of this small but growing cabal who are trying to quietly and unsanctimoniously live upright, decent lives. Seems like an appealing goal, but it's less common than one would hope. Bringing Epictetus back from the dead has been a surpassingly gratifying experience, and I hope that his helpful guidance will inspire and provide solace to the large audience of readers his brilliant thought deserves.

Why Would Anyone Want to Be a Stoic?

Sharon Lebell

If you were to introduce yourself to others by brightly declaring, "Hi, I'm a Stoic!" chances are, you probably wouldn't get too many dates. Stoics could do with better publicists and handlers, as their name is unfortunately tainted by ignorance and misunderstanding. When I've asked people what comes to mind when I ask them to picture a person who is a Stoic, I usually get a description of someone who sounds like they belong with the sphinx-like statesmen immortalized at Mount Rushmore. Grim, solemn, and humorless are the common descriptors. No cheer. No joy. No fun. No wonder Stoicism lacks cachet.

But are these descriptors true? Are they fair? And if they are worthy of our consideration, even as caricature, then why would anyone in their right mind want to be a Stoic? Furthermore, what might the ancient philosophy of Stoicism offer to us moderns? Why might Stoicism still matter and be of use to us in the twenty-first century?

To answer these questions, we need to explode a few myths about Stoicism: what it is, what it isn't, and what the allure of Stoicism's philosophy really is. This is a tall order for a short piece, but let's give it a try.

First, let's get it straight about what Stoicism isn't. It's not an injunction to merely "suck it up" in the face of pain or adversity. It's not a

Plus: Insights, Interviews, and More

fancy word for emotional repression or uptight reserve. To be fair, there is a moral sternness and rectitude to Stoic theory that might, at first blush, seem at odds with the emotionally impulsive, where's-the-next-big-fun culture we live in. However, Stoic ethics are, in fact, perfectly compatible with the ideals most of us honestly harbor for ourselves and for humanity. For example, many of us have become well adapted to thriving in a dog-eat-dog, get-what's-yours-and-run world. We have learned our moves and have well-managed public selves who efficiently advance and protect our interests. But that's not how most of us really want things to be. Certainly that's not the whole story.

I think that deep down, most of us wish we could handle the necessary transactions of life and not get brought down negotiating the anomie that characterizes our twenty-first century lives, while perhaps living in a more trusting, courteous, generous, and civil world. But most of us are not willing to be the foolish innocent who goes first. No one wants to be the chump. No one wants to work too hard. It's not that we're lazy. Most of us are just afraid, terrified of life's uncertainties.

Thus, most of us conduct ourselves as ostensibly good people, maybe not exceptionally good people, but sufficiently good, plausibly good. Our thoughts, words, and deeds conform to the socially acceptable moral standards that maintain friendships, propel commerce, and prevent civil disorder. Meanwhile, we privately pine for and often feel a strange nostalgia for what can only be called, however quaintly, virtue.

The Stoics understand that what we moderns experience as free-floating anxiety, the chronic longing for true intimacy, rootlessness and purposelessness, or an unquenchable sense of loss is really the consequence of our self-exile from virtue and its pursuit. And this is where the Stoics come in and have something to offer us. Stoics are unabashedly in the virtue business. To join the ranks of the Stoics is to cross over to valuing virtue over being cool, over being self-defensive, over playing it safe. Stoicism sees virtue as being uniquely and unconditionally a good. Other goods, such as friendship, kindness, love, or beauty, are extremely valuable, but only conditionally good. Virtue reigns supreme. And virtue is the way home to ourselves and to a truly engaged sense of belonging to others. The Stoic asks us to trade our hip ironic removal from ourselves and others for freedom from the ineffable sorrow, loneliness, fatigue, and self-doubt that dog us. Not a bad bargain.

But, this still might sound demanding, maybe too much so for us mere mortals. Who among us would want to embark on such a morally strenuous effort as the cultivation of virtue? Sounds great, but it also sounds really difficult. Onerous and not fun at all. Again, why would anyone want to be a Stoic? There are many reasons—good ones, in fact. Yet we must remember there are also a lot of Stoicisms. There is the Stoicism of Zeno of Citium, Stoicism's founder (ca. 335–263). There's the Stoicism of Chrysippus of Soli (c. 280–207 BC). Moving into the common era, there are the Stoicisms of Musonius Rufus (first century AD); Epictetus himself; and the

Roman emperor Marcus Aurelius (161–180 AD). Hellenists divide Stoics into four chronological periods: the Early Stoa (300–150 BC); Middle Stoa (150–55 BC); Late (Roman) Stoa (first century BC–third century AD); and Neostoicism (1584 AD–today). The Stoicism of Epictetus was a particularly therapeutic-oriented version of Stoicism, yet it is best understood within the larger theoretical framework it shares with other Stoicisms. Just as our social and inner emotional worlds are not tidy and univocal systems, Stoicism and Stoic ethics are not, either. But there are identifiable shared currents and coherences amongst them all. All these Stoicisms share the same allure: they offer a philosophy of emotional management in service of enduring inner peace and happiness.

Stoicism's beliefs offer comfort and embolden the human spirit without having to sacrifice reason. Quite the contrary. Unlike some religions, which require reason to be subordinated to faith, reason (*logos*) is the starting point for Stoic faith and the strength and endurance such faith provides.

There are several common inevitable human conditions, disturbances, or what the Stoics might call diseases of the soul for which Stoicism offers excellent remedies.

First off, one of these days, and it may have happened already, life is going to get you. It's going to broadside you somehow. No one, rich or poor, is spared. Life gives. Life takes away. Chances are, if it hasn't happened already, you're going to lose something or someone who is inordinately precious to you. Maybe it will be a home, a job, a marriage, a friend, your prized possession, your sense of self-worth, your mobility, your dignity, your health, or something else, and you're going to need to figure out how to carry on and make a good and meaningful life in the wake of and in spite of that potentially withering loss. Stoicism can be a steady, trustworthy companion during such times, a beacon that lights the way to the other side of despair.

Many of us come to a point in our lives when we have the persistent feeling that we have somehow betrayed our younger, more vital, expansive self by giving into a life of enforced duty or repetitive uncritical action. We feel caught, like we are violating our destinies, ignoring or even desecrating our own best natures and leaving our better selves behind. Our attention has become divided and fragmented, and from time to time we feel a summons to live in harmony with our nature, but we are at a loss for how to begin that journey home to ourselves, home to virtue. Stoic philosophy can reveal our better selves to us and lead us gently, by degrees, back to it.

Or perhaps we find ourselves robotically living out of cultural norms that we come to realize are based on false beliefs. Stoicism is superb at exposing the social fallacies and personal delusions that hinder our ability to feel connected to others, that undermine meaningfulness, or that reward the trivial at the expense of the vital and true. Stoicism teaches us to distinguish between true satisfaction and mere gratification, between self-reliant joy and nervous promiscuous acquisition, between peace of mind and twitchy, hollow ambition.

Plus: **Insights, Interviews, and More**

Finally, why does this ancient philosophy of Stoicism continue to matter in the twenty-first century, perhaps more now than ever before? Stoicism is a philosophy that, above all, teaches us how to make wise choices among an avalanche of choices. And, isn't that what we've got now? Choices up the kazoo. Because of information technology and worldwide connectivity, in a very short time we have had to adapt to a mind-numbing amount of inputs and options in any given day. This deluge of choice did not come with a manual for managing it. So we're winging it, which amounts to most of us yielding to, responding to, or engaging with those inputs that are the most familiar, loud, or persistent, rather than stepping back to sort and evaluate in terms of worthiness and value, which is to say, virtue. Epictetus's Stoicism offers us much, but above all, it is a terrific guide for cutting through our choice-saturated numbness and bewilderment in order to direct our attention to the things and people that really matter. Stoicism vets our choices of thought, word, and deed to help us live clear-sighted, ennobled lives and—yes, virtuous lives.

About the Editor

Sharon Lebell is a philosophical writer and performing musician who lives in Northern California. She is the author of
Naming Ourselves,
Naming Our Children,
and co-author of
The Music of Silence